# Brit Mu Briefly

## From Seeds to Civilization

© Copyright 2012.  Mfg Application Konsulting Engrg (MAKE)
All rights reserved.  Teachers may copy this book for school use.
ISBN  978-1-62495-016-2

Front Cover is the courtyard of the British Museum
Back Cover is the entrance to the British Museum

Through objects, we connect with our history. We touch how the past permeates the present.

These few pages are dedicated to the over ten thousand years of human history shown in the British Museum (Brit Mu).

May we learn to not repeat dark ages and to perpetuate the progress.

# Contents

| Topic | Description | Page Number |
|---|---|---|
| Pre-History | Crops | 1 |
| Pre-History | Cows | 2 |
| Pre-History | Cuneiform | 3 |
| Egyptian | Pyramids | 4 |
| Egyptian | Preserved | 5 |
| Egyptian | Papyrus | 6 |
| Greek | People-Centered | 7 |
| Greek | Pottery | 8 |
| Greek | Parthenon | 9 |
| Roman | Conquerors | 10 |
| Roman | Concrete | 11 |
| Roman | Culture | 12 |
| Dark Age | Kingdoms | 13 |
| Dark Age | Converts | 14 |
| Dark Age | Constricted - Learning | 15 |
| Renaissance | Relearn from Past | 16 |
| Renaissance | Race for Knowledge | 17 |
| Renaissance | Reason and Truth | 18 |
| Modern | From Seeds to Civilization | 19 - 21 |
|  | Summary | 22 |
|  | Credits |  |

# Pre-History                                    >8,000 BC

- Crops

Thousands of years ago, people in the Fertile Crescent learned how to farm. They grew **crops** of wheat and barley. They used stone and later bronze tools to plant the seeds and harvest the crops.

Pre-History                                    ~ 7,000 BC

- Cows

They also domesticated animals like **cows**, sheep and pigs. It was easier to raise animals than to hunt for them.

# Pre-History    -2,600 BC

- Cuneiform

People traded crops and cows.  Numbers were made to count the transactions.  The people of the Fertile Crescent also invented wedge shaped writing called **cuneiform**.

Irrigation caused salt build up on the land.  The soil was also depleted by over-planting.  Environmental disasters and wars caused these civilizations to decline.

# Egyptian                                    2,700 - 31 BC

- Pyramids

People traded the flora and fauna west to Egypt. The soil near the River Nile was very productive. The human population exploded. People could do different jobs other than farming.

The Pharaoh was the absolute ruler of the Egyptians. He organized the people to build massive stone monuments. The **pyramids** were part of the Pharaoh's plan for eternal life.

# Egyptian                                    2,700 - 31 BC

- Preserved

Egyptians **preserved** their dead royalty and religious leaders through mummification.  Egyptians believed that a mummy was prepared for the afterlife.

# Egyptian                              2,700 - 31 BC

- Papyrus

**Papyrus** is a reed that grows near the Nile. Egyptians made it into a type of 'paper' for their book-like scrolls. Try standing like the Egyptian in this picture. The feet are in-line on the side; torso front on, head turned and eye forward.

Greek Alexander the Great conquered Egypt in 332 BC. After Alexander died, Greek General Ptolemy and his family ruled Egypt until 31 BC when the Romans invaded.

# Greek                                                 480 - 86 BC

- People-centered

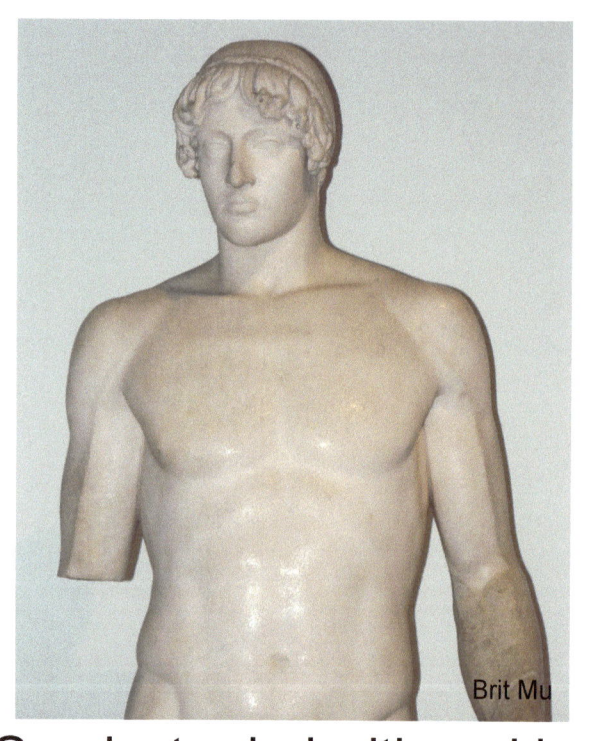 

Greeks traded with and learned from the Egyptians. The Greeks of Athens had lots of olive trees. They made olive oil. In their free time, the Greeks liked to think and reason. They created **people-centered** arts and philosophy. Greek statues looked life like. Greek gods looked like people. The Greeks also made a new form of government called democracy or people power. The people voted for their own rulers and government officials.

# Greek  480 - 86 BC

- Pottery

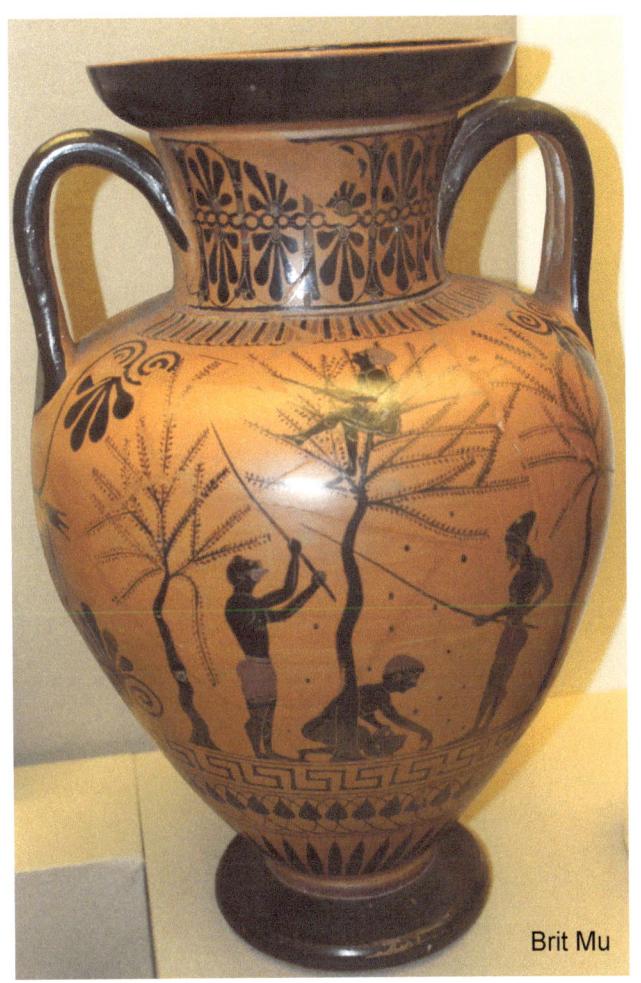

The Greeks made **pottery** to hold olive oil and wine etc. They traded their ceramics and idea around the Mediterranean Sea.

# Greek    480 - 86 BC

- Parthenon

The Greeks made a temple called the **Parthenon**. It was dedicated to worshiping Athena, the goddess of wisdom, peace and war.

Greek Civil War weakened the classical City-States. The Romans conquered Greece in 86 BC. Greece was not an independent country again until 1832 AD.

# Roman                                    500 BC to 476 AD

- Conquerors

Romans **conquered** millions of people living around the Mediterranean Sea from Britain to Turkey.
Romans assimilated the best from the cultures they took over. Romans copied the art, science and religion from Greece. They took the Greek gods and gave them new names. For example, Zeus became Jupiter.

# Roman                          500 BC to 476 AD

- Concrete

Romans discovered **concrete** and used it to build roads, aqueducts and massive public building. Roman houses had indoor plumbing.

11

# Roman  500 BC to 476 AD

- Culture

Roman marriage — Brit Mu

A B C D E F G H I K L M N O P Q R S T V X Y Z

Roman **culture** including the alphabet, laws and courts spread around the Mediterranean. We still use them today.
Low birthrate, lots of political infighting and a large number of enemies led to the Roman's decline. The Roman Empire ended when the city of Rome was attacked and sacked by barbarians in 476 AD.

# Dark Ages  < 500 - ~1500 AD

- Kingdoms

For the next 1000 years after the Roman Empire fell, Europe was in the Dark Ages. People still made significant items like this helmet but much knowledge was lost. People stopped progressing.

What had been one Roman Empire became many separate countries. Each small **kingdom** had their own King. Wars were frequent.

# Dark Ages      < 500 - ~1500 AD

- Converts

Christian and Muslim religions gained many **converts** during this time. Most people were illiterate. Christian Monasteries and Muslim libraries were the main repositories of knowledge. Literate Monks copied books by hand.

# Dark Ages      < 500 - ~1500 AD

- Constricted learning

Tommoso Laueti - Triumph of Christianity

Muslims were technologically more advanced than the Christian nations. In the West, people stopped being curious and **constricted learning**.
A person living in 500 AD would have noticed little change in the day to day life in the year 1500 AD. The Dark Ages gradually ended with the Renaissance.

# Renaissance                            >1400 AD

- Relearn from past

Raphael - The School of Athens

In Europe of the 1400's, there was a renewed interest to **relearn** from the past. Classical Greek and Roman knowledge became popular again. Much of the data came from Monasteries and Muslim libraries. This Rebirth of leaning is called the Renaissance.

# Renaissance                >1400 AD

- Race for Knowledge

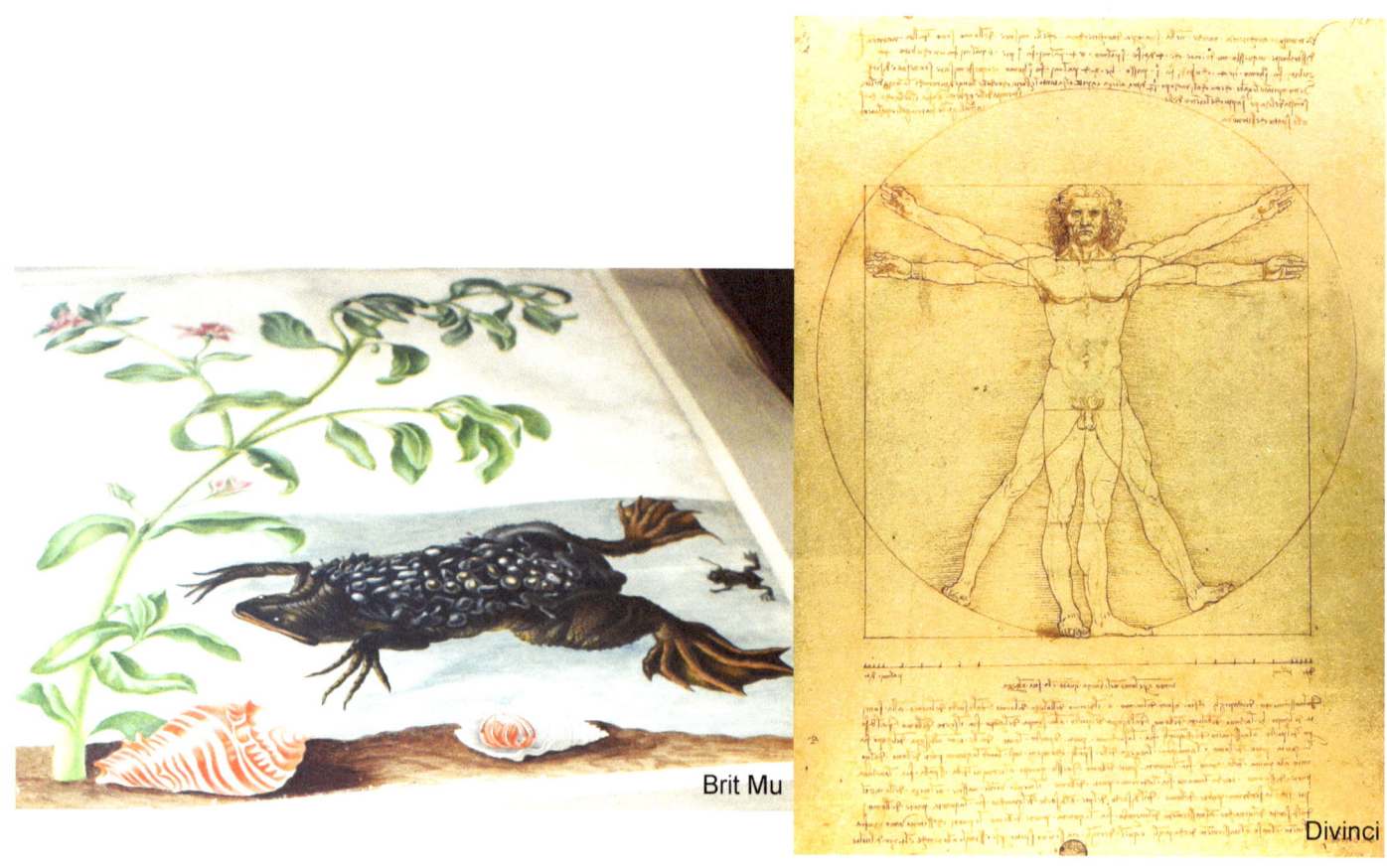

There was also a **race** for new knowledge. The arts and sciences flourished again.

Renaissance                                    >1400 AD

## • Reason and Truth

Through time, the ability to read Egyptian hieroglyphics was lost.
In the 1800's, the Rosetta Stone was discovered. It has the same message written in 3 languages. Scientists figured out how to read hieroglyphics again.

Enlightened people are curious. The search for **reason** and truth to understand and explain our world continues today.

Modern                                                          Today

• Signs

# A, B, C's

Morphy Richards 1980 Toaster

Wikipedia

Modern life is full of signs of our collective past.

Modern                                              Today

- Seeds

For example, the source of a beef sandwich is Fertile Crescent seeds and cows.  Sixty seconds, minutes and a seven day week came from the same place.
We owe our form of Government to the Greeks and our alphabet to the Romans.  The Romans based their alphabet on the Greeks who got the idea from the Phoenicians.

# Modern                                    Today

## •Civilization

It has taken thousands of years of human objects and experiences to get our civilization where it is today. In the hustle and bustle of our busy lives, there are echoes of the past everywhere.

# Summary

**PRE-HISTORY**
- Crops
- Cows
- Cuneiform

**EGYPTIAN**
- Pyramids
- Preserved-Royals
- Papyrus

**GREEK**
- People-centered
- Pottery
- Parthenon

**ROMAN**
- Conquerors
- Concrete
- Culture

**DARK AGES**
- Kingdoms
- Converts
- Constricted-learning

**REBIRTH AND ENLIGHTENMENT**
- Relearn from past
- Race for knowledge
- Reason and Truth

**MODERN**
- Signs
- Seeds
- Civilization

# Credits

We would like to thank the British Museum in London. Pictures in this books identified with "Brit Mu" were taken at the British Museum

Unless otherwise specified, pictures are in the public domain.

We would also like to thank www.wikipedia.org

**All Are Equal** – From Slavery to Civil Rights
**Brit Mu Briefly** - From Seeds to Civilization
**Catch Phrase Come-Froms** - Origins of Idioms
**Chase to Space** – The Space Race Story
**Civil Sense** – What if There Wasn't a Civil War?
**Common Come-Froms** – Origins of Objects
**Computer Come-Froms** –To Count, Compute & Connect
**Computer Patterns** – A Ditty on Digital
**Cozy Clozy** – From Fibers to Fabrics
**Essence of America** – The I's in US
**Essence of Science** – 7 Eye Opening Ideas
**Fishi and Birdy** - A Fable of Friends
**G Chicken & 5 K's** - The Thai Alphabet
**Images in Action** - Why Movies Move

Books are also available at http://www.lulu.com
Please contact us at:   trythaiketco@gmail.com

**Meaning of Money** - The American Way
**Nature's** Links of Life
**Ogs, Zogs and Useful Cogs** – A Tale of Teamwork
**Paintings With Insects, Eggs & Oils** – An Intro to Art
**Robin's First Flight** – Wings of Courage
**Skylings** – An Intro to Airplanes
**Stars of Days & Months** – The Story of 7 and 12
**Turtle Jumps** - A Tale of Determination
**Where Cookies Come-From** - From Dough to Delicious
**Who Did What in World History?** Past Echoes in the Present
**Why is California Interesting?** – Dreams of Gold
**Why is England Interesting?** – Worldwide Words
**Why is Thailand Interesting?** – Source of the Smiles
**Why is the USA Interesting?** - The 50 State Quarters

Books are also available at http://www.lulu.com
Please contact us at:   trythaiketco@gmail.com

**Recommend further reading:**

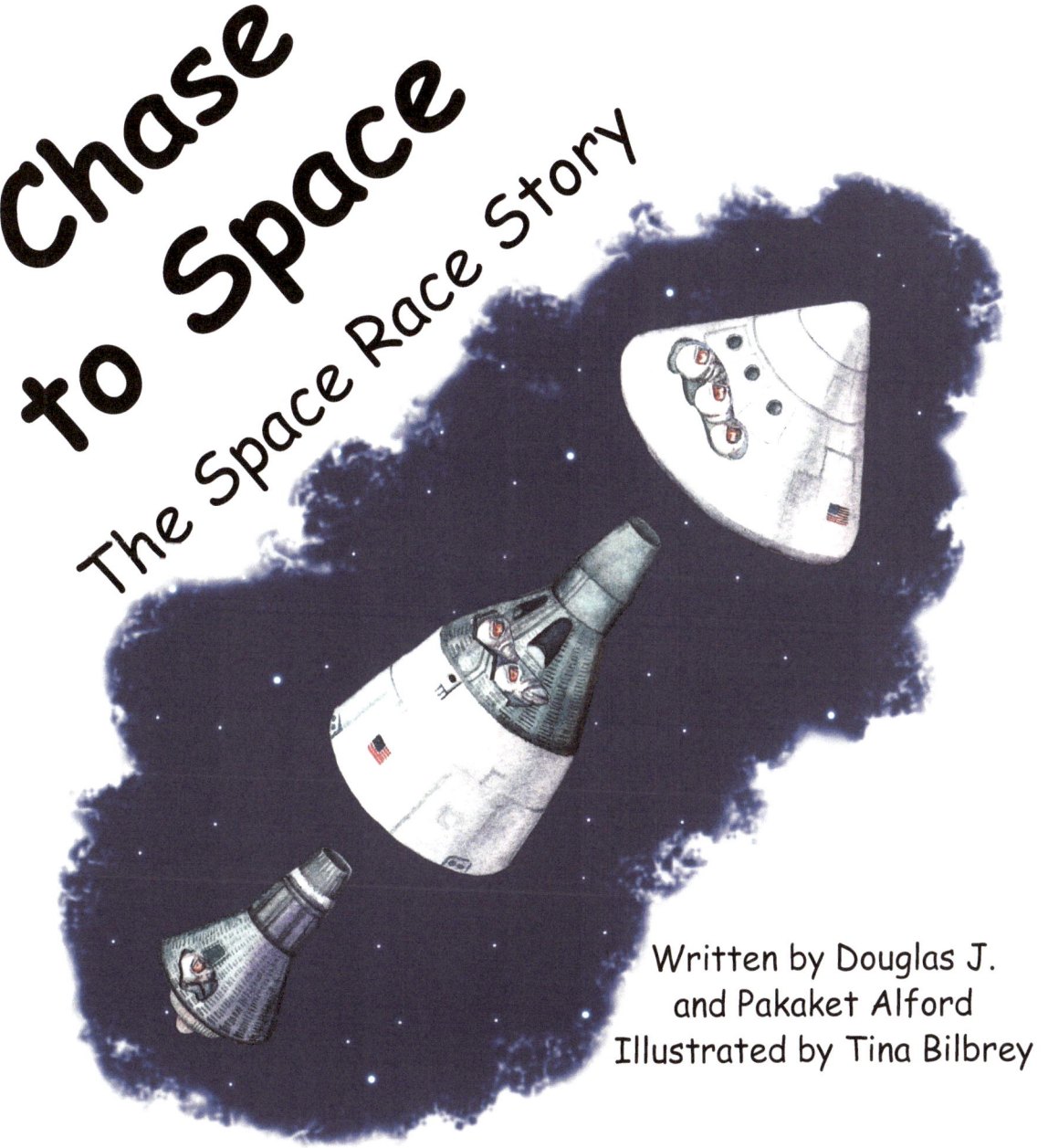

# Chase to Space
## The Space Race Story

Written by Douglas J.
and Pakaket Alford
Illustrated by Tina Bilbrey

# Nature's Links of Life

Douglas J. and Pakaket Alford

# Essence of Science
## - 7 Eye Opening Ideas

Douglas J. and Pakaket Alford

# Sky-Lings:
## An Intro to Airplanes

Douglas J. and Pakaket Alford

# Turtle Jumps!

Written by Douglas J. & Pakaket Alford
Illustrated by Tami Ashby

www.ingramcontent.com/pod-product-compliance
Ingram Content Group UK Ltd.
Pitfield, Milton Keynes, MK11 3LW, UK
UKHW061139180426
11947UKWH00002B/9